SARAH MOREY

The Art of Surviving You

Hope you enjoy

Sarah +

AUSTIN MACAULEY PUBLISHERS™

LONDON • CAMBRIDGE • NEW YORK • SHARJAH

A CIP catalogue record for this title is available from the British Library.

ISBN 9781398460508 (Paperback)
ISBN 9781398460515 (ePub e-book)

www.austinmacauley.com

First Published 2022
Austin Macauley Publishers Ltd
1 Canada Square
Canary Wharf
London
E14 5AA

DEDICATION

Firstly, to my nan and grandad for being the light in my dark days with the ability to make me smile no matter what.

My parents for supporting me through my life.

And to all the people who feel these chapters.

ACKNOWLEDGEMENTS

A huge thanks to a talented illustrator – Tom Hansler

POEMS

Adora

Scent

I feel safe
In your scent,
In your eyes,
You hold me close.
Cage me up,
But don't lock me in.

Set me free
If I need,
But keep me safe
In your shirt.

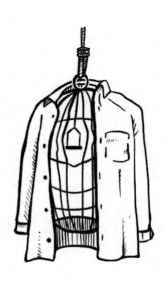

Body

My blemishes are constellations,
My curves mountains.

My mind is a maze,
Only some can beat.

My eyes are a mirror
But the one-way kind
I can see out –
You can't see in.

Monster

Toe heel, toe heel
The quick pace
Pitter patter.

Halt at the door.
Stare.
Into the darkness,

Quiet breath
Heavy. Steady,
Sleep.

The cold metal of the handle
Skin brushes.
Don't wake them.

Gently,
Squeak
Turn,
Pitter.
Patter.

Shatter of the night
Mummy,
Daddy
The big mean monster
Is coming to get me.

Aurora

Outside

Your eyes capture mine,
Your lips press deeply into me.
Your hands grab my waist
Digging in to hold me tighter.

From the outside.

I can't escape.
I try to run but
You've locked me in.
You suck the air from my lungs,
I'm no longer breathing.
Your claws dig into my skin,
Ready to rip me if I flee.

Like her

Does my hair not fall the right way?
Do my eyes not hold the right light?

                                    Like hers.

Do my lips not kiss you enough?
Do my hands not hold you right?

                                    Like hers.

Does my body not have the right shape?
Do my boobs not sit pretty enough?

                                    Like hers.

Do I need to scratch my face off?
Restart to be something new?

                                    Like her.

Just a little

Sweat sticks,
Lips bite
Fingers dig.

You dig, just a little too deep.

Teeth clank,
Hands roam
Toes curl.

I fall, just a little further.

Fault

Day by day
You watch me fade

As I take the blame
For your mistakes

Dionysus

Perhaps I overdosed on Dionysus –
He took my brain.
You and he are alike.

One sip too many
And I am yours to control,
Take me
And I can't say no.

I gave myself away
Finding solidarity
In a poison

Take my limbs
Tie the string,
Pull me to you
And I can't escape.

Perhaps I overdosed on Dionysus
Gave myself to him.

He promised to look after me.

You and he are alike
A step too many
In the wrong direction
And I can't turn back now.

Flaws

I know my flaws,
You do too.

But you've discovered more
The ones I hadn't seen

The way I speak,
Think,
Feel,
Breathe.

Maybe the way
I love is too smothering
My brain works is too messy,
I fell too hard for you
Or I breathe too heavy.

Storm

You haven't just clouded my brain.

You've collected the clouds,
Sparked the lightning,
Screamed out the thunder.

You started the storm inside my head.
The waves crash
Against my skull,
Batter my brain,
And flood my thoughts until I . . .
Can't breathe.

I can't breathe.
I can't speak.
I'm trapped inside the
Storm.

When I'm sad

When I'm sad,
I write.

When you're sad,
You
Call me names,
Replace my face,
Down the drink,
And blame it on me.

When I'm sad,
I tell you.

When you're sad,
You
Kick me whilst I'm down
Seek love in someone else,
And
Blame me.

Tear me up

Grip
Ripping me from the inside
My lungs burst
Explode
Fold
Stop.

I gasp.
Reach.
Scream
But nothing happens

My skin, my mind

My skin.
Touched, scarred, bruised.
Hidden to blind eyes,
Hidden by my lies.

My mind.
Touched, scarred, bruised.
Hidden to everyone,
Broken by you.

I won't tell (Part 1)

Sleep,
He can't hurt you.

Close your eyes,
He won't touch you.

Stay quiet,
He'll understand you.

Please,
      Stop.
            I won't tell.

Cecilia

Welcome

You wipe your feet on me,
Welcome home.

You climb on top of me,
Welcome in.

You wash your sins in me,
Welcome back.

I tell you I'm overused,
Goodbye.

Toxic

You breathe the toxic into my mouth
Down my throat,

Through the valves of my heart
Into the pit of my stomach.

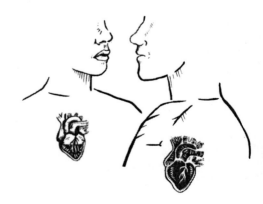

Oceans

Your eyes are my sun
Your body the ocean,
And your words the creatures

Sun burns,
Oceans drown,
And animals seem innocent
But rip each other apart
Just to survive.

Leave me alone

If I smash
My head against the table,

Will your poison
Just fall out?

Drunk

I drink
    And drink
     And drin k
      And dri nk
      I'm d r unk.

It's   not
easier
But it's

 easier

?

It's

                 not

 better
But it's even
 worse than
 before

Did I mention

Im drunk
?

You(')r(e) Poison

Your words work slowly,
Your name enters my eyes,
Your words attack my nerves,
Your past becomes my present.
Our past becomes my present.

Your life takes over mine,
Your poison weakens my thoughts
I can no longer be me.

Drunk Love

I only drunk love you,
When the venom
Invades my veins,

My brain isn't connected . . .

I love you.

I miss my life

I miss my life when you were just
A name,
A face,
A picture on the screen.

I miss my life when you couldn't
Bruise me;
My heart,
My thighs,
My brain.

I miss life before
I used alcohol to
Wipe your name off my lips,
Poison the feelings in my heart,
Silence the pain in my head.

I miss my life before
You ripped the real me away –
Injected your toxic lies into my mind,
Stabbed your knife into my heart,
And ripped me into a thousand pieces.

Because now I've learnt –
That no one can piece me together again.

Now you're a nightmare,
A reality.
A constant weight that crushes me,
Everything in my path.

Rock Bottom

Slices through my flesh,
Beat me 'til I'm blue, and
Purple and black and dead

Fill my lungs, your words turn to water
And drown me
Pull tears from my eyes, turn them red.
The anger you hold,
Hold against my neck.

Choke me of the love I feel for you.

I thought I fell down here,
But you pushed me
Down
To
Rock
Bottom.

Me or You

Empty, hollow
Your words echo.

Bound and chained,
You become the pain.

Pushed and pulled,
Please just hold

Me

Twisted and torn
I'll begin to mourn

You.

Red Rum

Red rum
From this liquor
Eats my veins
This poison works quicker.

Red rum
From your lips
Chews my heart
My soul – it splits.

Red rum
In the night
Creep on in
Turn out the light.

Murder
I drink.

You bite.
I die.

Goodbye.

Holes

You are in me
She is in you.
You push my walls,
Break through my body

She breaks through your walls
Something I could never do
Her eyes roam your body
As you open for her

You whisper the words
You think I want to hear
In a hushed husk
The moaning in my ear.

To the third person
The second girl
The one you want in this,
The images you build

Of a face that's not mine
With a body you've not yet roamed.
A land and sea that you will cover
As I watch upon the shore.

On my own ship
You call out to me,
But upon arrival
The wind carves her name
Into mine as it crashes

Onto me
like a
Tsunami.

Like you onto my body
Covering me in tainted
You.

My body crushed,
Crumbles into the satin floor
The sand turns to sheets,
The water turns to tears

As you wipe my body
Cleaning it from your mark
I wipe myself,
Layer up my body
As I sit in the room alone
Writing these words
Your mind filled with light
As mine sits in the dark.

Do you love me for me?
Or do you love me for the holes?
The wounds you've dug into me?

The holes

You force into
Shout into
Breathe into

The tainted waters
You splash upon me
Cover my senses,
So all I can do
Is love you.

Remain

I have let you go
But you still hold the reins
The strings on my limbs
The cage around my brain.

I may have set you free
But you remain
Crowd my brain
Whisper in my ear
I'm not good enough –
Not here.

You chain my trust to lies
My truth twisted to hate,

I fall onto him
But you catch me on the way down
Telling me he's not really there.

I'm a heavy weight,
Unable to be held.
You were strong
But not enough
For me.

I tried,
But not enough
For you.

Did you catch me?

Did you catch me?
Or are you
My puppet master –
Invisible strings.

Are you only here,
Because I tell you to,
Or are you here
Because I want
You to?

Marcella

I won't tell (Part 2)

Wake up,
He did that to you.

Open your eyes,
He hurt you.

Speak,
They'll believe you.

You're okay,
      You're safe now.
            He does not define you.

Push

I didn't fall out of love
With you,

I was pushed.

Pieces

When you're not around,
You are my imagination –
The good things
Pieced together
To create the perfect human.

But.

You bring the bad pieces
The pieces I didn't think fit,
The pieces I tried to forget –
The pieces from other puzzles,
I act like they don't fit.

But to you,
They're perfect.

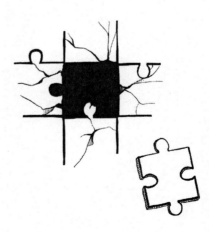

?

Trust?
Trust who?
Trust you?

Why?
You're different?
How so?

You're not him?

He wasn't either.

Another

You will love another –
You will cherish her flaws,
Forgive her past,
Give her your heart
And let her wander free.

And on that day
You will realise
That you never really loved me.

Next

To the next girl –
Be careful.

He blooms as a butterfly,
Morphs into an adder,
Attacks like a bull,
Screams like a fox.

He cocoons himself –
Don't wait for the change,
He spreads his wings
And flies away.

Vipera berus.
Tread carefully;
He bites when touched.

Spanish fighter.
Don't enter the cage;
No one can pull you out
Once he's trapped you against the fence.

Swift fox.
You claim your territory,
He seeks new land –
He won't stay long.

He is the wildlife
That will fend for itself.
Love until threatened,
And attack with venom.

Lie

You want me to hate you.
So here.
Here is the middle finger,
The fuck you
To you
To everything we ever had.

Fuck you for finding someone new.
Screw you for the attacks at night.
And fuck this, for wasting my time
And crushing me.

You want me to hate you.
So here.
The hate for screwing my brain
My heart and my body.
I despise you for taking me,
Holding my heart against yours
And squeezing it for
Everything I have

And here is the hate
Because I still love you
I still fall
Into those toxic eyes,
For the constructed lies
And the way your voice sounds
When you tell me we'll be alright.

I hate you
For the lie
That we
Will be
Alright.

One Night

I spent a night with him.
But not one of passion.
His skin never touched mine,
Fingers never traced my curves,
He never lay inside me.

But he covered me
In his words,
In the promises you never kept.
His lips never touched mine
But my heart was held.

I soaked my words in salted tears –
He let me reap you
From my soul and my heart.

His heart never collided with mine.
That night,
It greeted me
With open arms
A kind mind,
And a certainty of safety.

I thought

I thought I had to teach myself
How to trust,

I thought I had to trust
And talk to people,

I thought I had to talk to people
About how I feel.

I feel
I need
To change
My expectation.

I understand that I put
Them
First
Therefore, I have no choice
But to come
Second.

I will be
Second place
Second thought

Third thought

Last thought

Forgotten.

Recovery

"Recovery"
Is scary.

Does it even exist?
Or will I be
Broken forever,
Drinking forever,
Scared forever.

All I know,
Is that one thing exists –

(I've tasted it, once or twice)

Surviving.

And I promise,
I will survive you.

It's my art.

ABOUT THE AUTHOR

Sarah Morey is a creative writing and publishing graduate and has been writing poetry all her adult life. She is passionate about the creative industries and she carries this into her baking, posting her creations to Instagram. She also translates her expertise into the marketing industries, connecting businesses to audiences.

Alongside her passions, she speaks out for mental health awareness and standing up for those who may be unable to stand up for themselves – who she aims to reach through her poetry.